D0729049

# Danny Boy

# DANNY BOY
*The Beloved Irish Ballad*

# RUNNING PRESS
PHILADELPHIA • LONDON

A Running Press® Miniature Edition™

© 2002 by Running Press
All rights reserved under the Pan-American and International Copyright Conventions

Printed in China

*This book may not be reproduced in whole or in part, in any form or by any means, electronic or mechanical, including photocopying, recording, or by any information storage and retrieval system now known or hereafter invented, without written permission from the publisher.*

*The proprietary trade dress, including the size and format, of this Running Press® Miniature Edition™ is the property of Running Press. It may not be used or reproduced without the express written permission of Running Press.*

Library of Congress Cataloging-in-Publication Number 2001094114

ISBN 0-7624-1242-9

This book may be ordered by mail from the publisher. Please include $1.00 for postage and handling.
**But try your bookstore first!**

Running Press Book Publishers
125 South Twenty-second Street
Philadelphia, Pennsylvania 19103-4399

Log onto www.specialfavors.com to order
Running Press Miniature Editions™ with your
own custom-made covers!

Visit us on the web!
www.runningpress.com

# ENGLISH VERSION

# OH DANNY
## BOY, THE PIPES, THE PIPES ARE CALLING

---

# ƒROM GLEN
## TO GLEN AND DOWN THE
## MOUNTAIN SIDE

THE SUMMER'S
GONE AND
ALL THE
LEAVES ARE
FALLING

# 'TIS YOU,

## 'TIS YOU MUST GO AND I

## MUST BIDE.

---

# Βut come

## ye back when summer's

## in the meadow

# Or when
## THE VALLEY'S HUSHED
## AND WHITE WITH SNOW

16

# AND I'LL

## BE HERE IN SUNSHINE

## OR IN SHADOW

---

17

# oh danny boy, oh danny boy i love you so.

# $B$UT IF

## HE COME AND ALL
## THE ROSES DYING

---

20

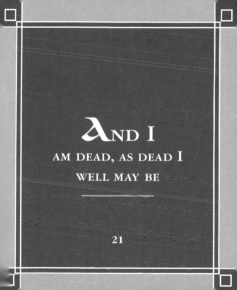

# And I

### AM DEAD, AS DEAD I

### WELL MAY BE

21

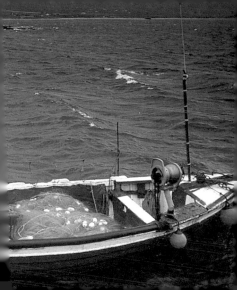

# hE'LL COME
## HERE AND FIND THE
## PLACE I'M LYING

---

# ᴀND KNEEL

## ᴀND SAY ᴀN ᴀVE

### THERE FOR ME.

# AND I shall feel, oh soft you TREAD ABOVE ME

# AND THEN

MY GRAVE WILL RICHER, RICHER

SWEETER BE

---

# fOR YOU

## WILL BEND AND TELL ME

## THAT YOU LOVE ME

---

# AND I SHALL REST IN PEACE UNTIL YOU COME TO ME.

# GAELIC
## VERSION

# Is é mo

## CHAOI GAN MISE

## MAIDIN AERACH,

---

36

# Amuigh i

## mBéarra i m' sheasamh

### ar an dtrá,

---

# Is guth

## NA N-ÉAN 'O M'

## THARRAING THAR NA

## SLÉIBHTE COIS NA

## FARRAIGE,

---

# Go Céim

## an Aitinn mar a

## mbíonn mo ghrá.

---

IS OBANN
AOIBHINN
AITEASACH
DO LÉIMFINN,

# Do rífinn

saor ó ana-bhroid
an tláis,

---

44

# Do THABHARFAINN

## DROIM LE SCAMALLAIBH

## AN TSAOIL SEO,

---

45

# IS NEART MO CHLÉIBH DÁ THACHTADH ANSEO SA TSRÁID,

# AN FHAD

TÁ RÉIM NA HABHANN

AGUS GAOTH GLAN

NA FARRAIGE

---

# Ag Glaoch

IS AR GAIRM AR AN GCROÍ

SEO I M' LÁR.

---

# ıs milis

## briomhar leathanbhog

## an t-aer ann,

---

# Ls gile

## ón ngréin go fairsing

## ar an mbán,

---

# IS OCHÓN,
# A RÍBHEAN
# BHANÚIL NA
# GCRAOBHFHOLT,

GAN SINNE
ARAON I
MEASC AN
AITINN MAR
DO BHÍMIS
TRÁTH!

# FRENCH
## VERSION

# Garçon, les

## Tuyau, les Tuyau

### Appelons

66

# De vallée

## à vallée, et en bas

## les versant de

## LA MONTAGNE

67

# Les été

VA, ET TOUTES LES
FLEURS MOURONS

70

# Vous, vous

## devoir vont et Je supporter.

71

# MAIS VIENS VOUS VERSO QUAND ÉTÉ DANS LES PRÉ

# Ou quand

## LES VALLÉE SILENCE ET
## PÂLE À NEIGER

---

# ÊTRE Y
## DANS SOLEIL OU
## DANS OMBRE

---

# Garçon, garçon, Je vous aime tellement.

---

# Et si

VOUS VENEZ, QUAND
TOUTES LES FLEURS
MOURONS

ET JE SUIS
MORT, QUE
MORT MOI
SAIN
MAI ÊTRE

# [Υου'll] viens
## et trouver la place où
### Je suis mentant

———

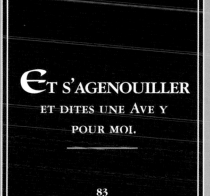

# ET S'AGENOUILLER

ET DITES UNE AVE Y
POUR MOI.

# Et moi écouter,

## TAMISÉE VOUS ÉCRASER

## EN HAUT MYSELF

---

# Et toutes

## Mon songer vouloir

### Réchauffer et sucrée être

# SI PAS
## échouer à
## dit myself
## thanksgiving
## vous aimez
# MOI

# MOI
## SIMPLEMENT SOMMEIL DANS TRANQUILLITÉ JUSQU À CE QUE VOUS VENEZ À MOI

## PHOTO CREDITS

THIS BOOK HAS BEEN
BOUND USING HANDCRAFT
METHODS AND SMYTH-SEWN
TO ENSURE DURABILITY.

THE DUST JACKET AND INTERIOR WERE
DESIGNED BY MATT GOODMAN.

THE TEXT WAS EDITED
BY MOLLY JAY.

THE TEXT WAS SET IN OMNIA,
GARAMOND3BOLD SC, AND
GARAMOND3 ITALIC OSF.